MOVE
WITHOUT THE
BALL

A Playbook for Success in Sports and Life

DR JANA HAYWOOD
ILLUMINE SOLUTIONS GROUP, CEO

Published in the United States, Mission Possible Press, a Division of Absolute Good Enterprises. AbsoluteGoodEnterprises.com

Illumine Solutions Group, LLC.
Illuminesolutionsgroupisg.com
janarhaywood@illuminesolutionsgroupisg.com

ISBN: 979-8-9910404-0-2

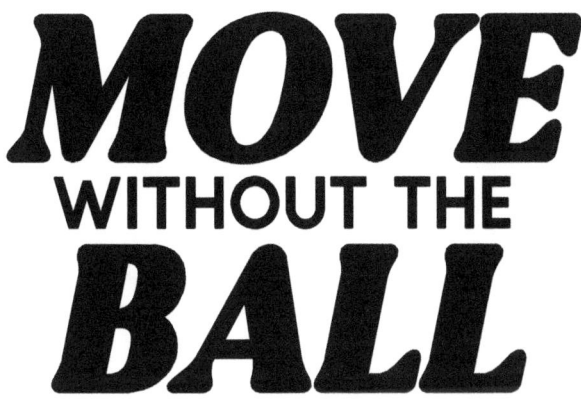

Dedication

To female ballers; past, present and future. Keep moving.

Acknowledgements

Carl, you are one of my life's greatest joys. Without you, I would not be able to move the way I do. Thank you for knowing us well enough to call the right plays at the right time.

Carl James, Jaila and Jordyn, thank you for showing me that in life parking a car is not the same as placing it in neutral. Thank you for giving me courage to go in reverse when needed and to drive until the wheels fall off. Thank you for keeping me moving.

To my parents, you are my first coaches and trusted confidants. Your wisdom continues to bless me.

Jay, my lifelong best friend, thank you for always showing up for me.

"Framily" is everything. I have learned that blood is not the determining factor for family. Success is so much sweeter when you have special people to share the journey. I am blessed to have many.

To my mentor and friend kind of, thank you for showing me how to Move Without the Ball by starting with loving myself so I can love others.

God, in You do I move and have my being. (Acts 17:28) I thank You.

Jana

Contents

Section One
Making Successful Moves

Athletic Advantage Is a Real Thing

The culture of sports carries into professional life and work culture. Women who lack the experience of being on a sports team may not be familiar with the way training, practicing, playing and performing in real time on teams has permeated the demands, expectations and success ratios of those who are considered "elite" or "successful" in their fields.

Athletes are coached, taught to grind, to compete and to win. Other professionals, and especially women, are not trained in the same manner, so the learning curve is different. When non-athletes are working in an environment with those who have "the sports advantage," it can be alarming, and shocking.

This book is important because I'm providing insight for women (and our young female athletes) - as a translator because the workplace (and successful spaces) are dominated by many competitive men, and former athletes.

Let's move!

Where Sports and Life Intersect

I was a sprinter and loved it - the freedom of running, and fast. Then one day I stopped. Recently, over 20 years later, I learned I'd had a chance to become a Junior Olympian in the high jump if I had cleared one more height. Instead, I chose basketball because I loved it more. I kept participating in basketball and eventually traveled the world playing the game I loved so much, for a time. At 18 years old, I'd gotten married to my husband, who had been a national indoor track and field champion himself. He wholeheartedly supported my athletic pursuits. In October 2004, I had my son. My husband and family cared for him, as I played another season. In April of 2005, I realized I could continue to play internationally, but wouldn't make the WNBA. I put down the ball.

Despite having an undergraduate degree in business, I now knew that I wanted to become a teacher, so I became one while going back to earn my first master's degree and becoming certified. I was working part of the day as a teacher and part of the day as the athletic director. I recognized I wouldn't achieve my professional goals if I remained attached to the sports director position. I moved without the ball. When I decided I wanted to move into a leadership role, I pursued a masters in administration; my first principalship soon followed. After holding the position of principal for a little more than a decade, I went back to school to obtain my doctorate in Educational Leadership, positioning myself for the pursuit of district leadership and outside opportunities. Recently, I have focused on human resources because of my passion around recruitment, development and building high functioning teams. No, it's not sports, but isn't everything? I always tell my kids, "life is school" and my girls say, "No mom, everything's not about school!"

Just like it would be easy to say life isn't about basketball... be forewarned, I can take about anything and put it into a sports analogy, and you'll get plenty of those as we move forward!

Life's Lessons

Life and sports have taught me many lessons. Academically, I was fortunate to achieve and professionally, I attribute much of my success to my participation in sports at a young age. In this short, focused work, I'm going to share some "plays" for you to achieve success - by Moving Without the Ball - a sports analogy that applies to life as well. Because if you stay stuck, you won't get the ball, and you won't win.

In track and field, I learned how to compete with my greatest competitor, myself. In track, you can compete in individual events, or you can choose to be part of a relay team. I didn't truly get the value of team until I was a track athlete... when doing it by myself, running the 400 meter dash, there was some satisfaction. Yet, when we ran and won the 4 x 400 meter relay as a team, it superseded reward. The shared satisfaction was nearly euphoric because I was part of something bigger than myself. I will never forget how Brandy taught me this lesson.

While at the state championship, she was the alternate on the 4 x 400 meter relay which meant coach could put her in the races leading up to and including the final if he chose to hold someone else out. Brandy was fast and capable of making sure the team made the times needed to make the championship race. She ran every race except the final so that I could rest my legs and compete in other events for the good of the team. I ran the final race replacing her and WE WON! We won the race and the Class 2A Missouri State

4

Track and Field Championship. Although I along with the other three girls in the race received the gold medal for the 4 x 400 meter dash that day, we all, including Brandy won as a team. I have never forgotten her sacrifice and willingness to put the team first; it changed me.

In track, there is no ball - so it's literally moving without the ball. You have a targeted, specific goal - reaching the finish line, first. The official starts the race, and you have a short window to win. If you have an off day, and you're unable to recover quickly, the consequence is yours when competing individually.

When you don't recover quickly on a relay team, it's shared accountability, you have to answer to your teammates - you either adjust or get replaced.

In basketball, you learn to endure changes in momentum because the game is longer - you're playing through quarters or halves - you must learn to withstand adversity (runs) and ride the shifts if success in the form of victory is to be reflected in the final score. Concurrently, teammates can pick up the slack/step in and up on your behalf. You're all focused on working together - Moving With the Ball, to get the win.

There will be times in life, you'll have to stand up for yourself, alone; facing yourself as your biggest competitor. At other times, you'll be able to win while having the support and momentum of others. Success in life is a choice. We are a compilation of all of our previous experiences. Nothing should be wasted. As you choose to customize your playbook, intentionally draw upon those previous experiences because they will be a major part of designing your life's success.

When you keep what's working for you and let go of what's not, choosing to develop skills, habits, and you focus on your plan, you will move forward - this is how you Move Without the Ball. It's exhilarating when you think about it! You get to design what success means to you. There's something really powerful about the freedom and joy of being aligned in life to love, work and whatever you deem is most important to you!

When you fail to be your fullest self, you're actually robbing not only yourself, but also those you are meant to influence. Be you! You are great!

Authenticity is Your Success!

Success in Life is Achieved While Doing Your Best Work

As you'll read, playing sports gave me a significant opportunity to apply the skills and experiences I learned to improve, significantly, in life. If you're a parent, one who is transitioning from college to professional life, and/or are wanting to achieve a new level of success, moving from where you are to where you hope to be, you've come to the right place. I'm here to assure you that you can get through each challenge and opportunity with intentional focus, determination and teamwork - the team you build to support your endeavors.

It is a beautiful sight to witness when an athlete, no matter the sport, is dominating their opponent on the competition field. Spectators and onlookers are mesmerized by the level of skill they are watching on display as the running back bursts through a hole, the hockey player swerves in and out of traffic, the volleyball player comes down on the ball at the apex of its ascension, and the basketball player crosses someone over so good that the defender loses balance as the offensive player shoots the rock and scores. Everybody loves it. The crowd goes wild!

What not everyone has a trained eye to see is what the players are doing on the floor or field when they don't have the ball. Great players are working as hard and probably harder when they are Without the Ball to get open and make sure the play runs as planned. They execute plays with precision and perfection: keeping the proper spacing, setting blocks/screens, making hard cuts and accelerating and decelerating as needed to get an advantage on their opponent.

Now, let's look even closer at the scene because a true fan or student of the game gets to the point that they can see the person with the ball doing their thing, those around them moving to execute the play, and also the defender who is looking to get the ball.

Sometimes you have to commit to as we say in basketball, 'locking someone down on defense' so you can get a stop or a steal.

When you get to the point that you are willing and excited about playing defense as hard as you play offense, you have transcended to the next level. **It is in that space you realize that you will only win the game if you play both ends of the floor.** It is a life lesson that catapults you from good to great.

None of us will always have possession of the ball or be on the offensive team. Getting the glory and spotlight provide instant gratification. Life isn't always that way. Life is going to deal you some cards that you hadn't expected, some disappointments and some hardships, and naysayers and haters. That's when having played gritty, sometimes scrappy defense pays off. Not all wins are pretty. In those moments, transcend. Get a stop (meaning, don't allow your opponent to score, gain momentum or get the advantage); Move Without the Ball. During these seconds or moments, you're using your basketball IQ to determine how you'll get positioned to get the ball back in hand, or support your teammate in doing so. Once you get the ball back, don't allow your hard work and perseverance to be in vain.

Living and Excelling

In life, you also have to utilize your emotional and professional IQ, so it's important to look around to determine what's your best next move. In periods of transition, you're moving without the ball, just like on the court.

Maximize your time by investing in your growth and development.

Reward, compensation and recognition occur when you Move with the Ball, when you have it. When it's not in your possession, Move Without the Ball to gain perspective and leverage by shifting and re-positioning.

Be the top performer in your current position and be in thought partnership with others on the field/court, and in your field. Ways to achieve this in life is by choosing:

Continued Education: Attending workshops, taking courses, earning certificates or degrees.

Enhancing Your Skillset by Engagement: Applying for apprenticeships, internships, requesting mentorship or hiring a coach.

Broadening Your Connections by: Attending networking events, joining professional organizations or volunteering to chair committees to gain and demonstrate leadership experience.

Now that we have a basic understanding, you get to...

Use your skills!
Execute your play!
Make things happen!
Do something significant whenever you have the opportunity.

Success in Life is Achieved While Doing Your Best Work!

Taking Your Shots

Practice, Preparation and Timing, Sports Analogies for Life

Why is it important to be able to Move Without the Ball?

You have to put yourself in position to get the ball. When you're standing still, your teammates can't see you and sometimes you take yourself out of the play by hiding behind other people or fading out of bounds. So, not only do you want to Move Without the Ball, you also want to move with purpose.

Try to catch the ball in the places where you are strongest - moving where you know you'll have success. Sometimes you're moving to set someone up on your team - you're moving so that your teammate can get open and make a big play while they have the ball. You run understanding good ball movement is how you will beat the defense.

Why is "Passing" Hindering Women's Success, Professionally?

It is because they don't know you have to Move Without the Ball to get the ball. It's not a negative thing to be a ball hog - women tend to share more than men, and when that happens, you are passing on your shot. It's okay to be an assist leader, but sometimes you have to take the shot. When you don't, you actually hinder the team and yourself.

In basketball, whenever you pass the ball, you should cut through (move). That creates distance between you and your defender, but also keeps spacing on the floor. You want spacing, so you can identify opportunities and then maximize them.

It's All About Strategy

You can't be someone who is only able to do a jump shot or a fast break layup. To be successful, you have to have a comprehensive skillset and be well-rounded. You must know when to take your shots, which means being in rhythm and prepared so when the door of opportunity presents itself, you are prepared to take it in a professional setting.

Bad shots are equivalent to sometimes wanting to move too quickly. Read the room. Too many times women have been preparing a proposal or significant idea and then someone "in the room" has stolen their intellectual property, presenting the material as if it's their own.

Learning on the job is a real thing - being in a job you're not prepared for can be a source of frustration and could bring about self-doubt, disappointment and maybe even cause you to lose credibility. Do not confuse this with imposter syndrome. You know what you know and what you don't.

Constantly having to reinvent yourself in your work means continuous improvement and changing your shot. How do you accomplish that? Go back to the beginning and learn more, gain new skills, get coaching, and keep improving. When you don't know something, the best investment that you can make is in gathering knowledge, making slight changes, overcoming injuries and being willing to adjust.

It can be injury like mine (more on that later), or reinventing yourself as a result of professionally focused career endeavors, or stages of life like managing marriage, motherhood, family dynamics, financial status challenges and the natural changes which happen during phases of life around aging.

And, if you've ever thought any of these things, it's okay; it's just time to regroup, and Move! *I'm working hard but not yielding the results. If you haven't quite been able to achieve the results you're looking for, take time to strategize what's necessary for you to get on track.*

I'm ready to transition from this position, but I'm not sure I want to give up what I have now to get there. Check in with your inner-most being and remember what ignites you - your purpose and vision are tied together.
I want my daughter(s) to make different choices than I did, and things are changing so quickly. She may not go pro, and I'm not sure how to guide and support her without ruffling feathers. Acknowledge your hesitation to put your desires onto her; ask what she needs and wants, then encourage her hopes, and help her work through fears. Work with her to come up with a game plan. We all have one life to live and must live it for ourselves. No re-dos.

And, if you've ever thought any of these things, it's okay; it's just time to regroup, and Move! I'm working hard but not yielding the results. If you haven't quite been able to achieve the results you're looking for, take time to strategize what's necessary for you to get on track.

Do not isolate!
Evaluate where you are and be open to moving.

Being coachable and making adjustments in real time to achieve goals is the way you become successful.

Consider what I shared in Chapter One and choose a path: **Continued Education, Enhancing Your Skillset by Engagement and Broadening Your Connections.**

Moving Toward Success

*What I learned about success in life was primarily
forged from my experience in playing basketball
beginning at the age of 12 and eventually becoming
an international player.*

What I Inherited

Unique to sports compared to other spaces, you get real time feedback that is applied in the moment. You get it from the coach who is observing, then giving you the feedback to make the adjustment immediately. You take the feedback and execute it and/or you discuss a better way to do it. Collectively, you choose what works and begin making adjustments - so you are refining the skill. This is an amazing process that benefits athletes, within the scope of games, practice, and in life.

Those who have not participated in sports have not necessarily developed the mindset and ability to receive feedback and adjust in the moment. Unfortunately, when it comes to the workspace, that's a disadvantage. There's a greater learning curve. When your supervisor is giving you feedback, coaching - *the feedback is a gift and can lead to you achieving a performance outcome* - difficulties can arise when you don't recognize or trust the feedback.

When you're resistant to being coached, that means you're interpreting it as a critique that is final as opposed to receiving information from someone who is mutually invested in your growth, development and goal attainment.

Willingness to Adjust

A person's ability to be coachable or flexible in the workspace often assists them in becoming more successful, and rise to greater levels. For those who have been in sports, continuous improvement is normalized as continuous improvement so you don't feel as offended because you are accustomed to feedback that is sometimes critical and hard to swallow.

Those in sports don't naturally or readily 'question the motives' of their coaches because it's usually clear - we're in this together, we have defined goals, and the coach is usually experienced and objective about how to bring out the best in the players, striving for the win.

If you've not participated in sports, okay. But now you have the advantage of insight and the ability to practice your skills while you Move Without the Ball.

Are you willing to make immediate adjustments?

Finding Your Sweet Spot

Often, when starting your career, you're trying to be who you think they want you to be. Over time you become "that at work" and "this at home" but over time you become your full-self at work and at home - bringing you wherever you go. That's when you are your best, being you is your sweet spot. People trust you - when the walls come down you do your best work.

Understanding people is a huge part of leadership. You need to know what makes a person on your team tick. Recognition and acknowledgement go a long way for women; yet, men often are motivated by power, roles, and money.

1.　　**Self-Love.** Create goals around your personal well-being. Build a social circle and have fun by separating from your professional network. It's a natural lean to be around others in your profession; however, you can be boxed into your role and become a prisoner to that persona.

　　　　Take off that mask and enjoy yourself; you deserve it.

2.　　**You are a resource, not the source!**

3.　　**Care about those you are leading.** We are all leaders, even when we don't have the titles!

4.　　**Leaders Make Decisions - They are often tough...**

5.　　**You Are Modeling What You Expect** - You are demonstrating the vision, whatever it is.

15

6. **Set Expectations** - For yourself and those in your charge so that people know what they're being measured against. If you are in a leadership role, provide coaching and training so that they are equipped to carry out that duty.

7. **Delegating** - Requires trust, training and finesse... have others see themselves as a valuable contributor to the overall role, and treat them as such. Yes, it's a big deal that you trust them, and you must not micromanage them. Micromanaging means you really don't trust them - so if you don't place it in their hands, that's up to you...

8. **Mistakes happen, don't let them define you.** Often, men get forgiven and get a pass - women often get chastised and blamed. It becomes about our "decision making capabilities." Don't take the bait. Buckle down and move on.

9. **Decision-Making** - Learn to read the defense and make real time decisions (decisions can be difficult) based off the skills you have; you're deciding in the moment what move to make.

10. **Roles** - Titles are good however, they don't necessarily define the role, and that can cause confusion. A leader plays all the roles if needed so don't get too big for whatever moves need to be made. If you have walked a mile in 'their' shoes, you wouldn't say certain things or act a certain way.

    Remember to be humble and responsible in the way you treat people even if you don't know the role or haven't had experience in it.

11. **Leap Frogging to the Top** - (Being put in the position) can cause a negative trickle down or top up effect. There is still a lot to be said about climbing or working your way up the rungs. When you lead you want someone to follow and that requires that they respect you. Knowing it (the leadership role) was not given to you but earned, garners points with your people.

12. **Responsibilities** - You can delegate the duty but not the responsibility. You are the leader. Choose wisely.

13. **Accountability** - It doesn't feel personal when expectations have been clearly communicated, established, and monitored.

14. **Over-Communicating** - Make things crystal clear. There is no grey when you tell them what you're going to tell them. Tell them, and then tell them what you told them.

Notes About Self-Care

Taking care of you is non-negotiable. You've probably heard some of the items I've listed before - but I'm emphasizing them because you can't care for others well if you don't care for yourself. You can't pour from an empty cup though many women attempt it daily... Investing in yourself means keeping your cup full, continuously. So remember to:

- Engage in exercise, get plenty of sleep, eat well, and take healthy supplements.

- Create Healthy Boundaries - This includes delegating when possible; utilizing support systems and team efforts; as well as adhering to scheduled work hours, quiet time (emails), lunch hours, and limits on additional projects.

  Saying "Yes" to everything else leaves you with "No" (time, space, energy or capacity) for yourself.

- Schedule "Me" Days - Massage, manicure, pedicure, rest, binge watch a series, read, enjoy staycations and travel when you can!

- Attend social hours with friends!

- Listen to great music and laugh out loud.

- Enjoy hobbies and make time for fun

- Spirituality, Meditation and Prayer are foundational to grounding, purpose and maintaining overall health. I highly recommend daily practice of each.

- Get a Therapist, Life Coach, Executive Coach and a great Medical Doctor. Seriously!

Making Tough Decisions

*As a professional, making tough decisions can be stressful
and difficult, yet it's necessary and required.*

A part of the job I don't necessarily enjoy is delivering what
feels like unfavorable news. Change is hard. Yet, when you
fail to take needed action, you're harming the organization
and maybe the individual.

I started to put off the meeting, knowing she was having
difficulty in her personal life. Then I thought no, let me not
put this off any longer because there was always going to be
something. Prolonging the inevitable makes a smaller issue
bigger because it grows.

You get to cash in on being a fair leader all the time – people
deserve to minimally be treated following the policy, yet
treating them well honoring their dignity and worth creates
a level of trust that when a tough decision is being made you
as the leader are not out to even a score, by being vindictive
or being power struck. People respect that as a leader.

19

Male Professionals Versus Female Professionals

Expectations vary and so do results!

Being a Female Professional Takes Grit and Twice the Effort

In speaking with other female professionals over the years, we've agreed that the way to "get things approved" by male leaders is to: *Smell good, look good, smile and stroke his/ their ego... it's the game you play.* Half of the time "he" may not hear what you are saying during the meeting, but as long as you do those four things, the answer is usually, "yes."

It's not easy to say it, nor do I necessarily like it, but it's a real thing, and unfortunate in today's climate. I'd like to be able to tell you that your degrees, dedication and hard work will be respected, appreciated and applauded because you've earned it and deserve it, yet, that's not often the case. The battle for workplace equity continues.

Recently, I had a conversation with a woman who would be considered a higher up. She talked about all of the little details that women have to consider that quite frankly men do not. *Am I standing too close to him? Should this be a handshake or a hug moment? Who else can I invite to dinner so it is not just the two of us? Does this outfit say smart, sexy or both? What will this audience appreciate the most? Is my nail polish too bold, heels too high, or hair too?* ...the list goes on and on. I don't believe it should be that way; however, it is. And we keep moving because we owe it to ourselves. We must honor the women who paved the way for us and illuminate the path for those young women coming behind us.

20

Knowing this and acknowledging it will help you prepare for the "fight" when it occurs and throughout your career. It's also another incentive to be intentional as you switch positions and move toward management or transition during any phase of your career. Representation matters.

Micro-Aggressions

As women we often experience micro-aggressions (sexism, classism, racism) in the workspace and in life. Men often try to manipulate women as if they are the superior sex, as if we are not clued in to what they are doing. They may give you a compliment about your physical appearance, how you smell or your facial expression, especially when you smile... all to distract or diminish the intellectual contributions you are making.

You may have given an award-worthy presentation at 10am and you didn't get a pat on the back, then 'he' sees your lunch full of leftovers and commends the way your plate is presented. *Why is it easier for him to acknowledge one and seemingly ignore the other?* Ego, male culture, pride, power playing... the list goes on. It's maddening, but a problem which continues.

Womanhood

Women are physiologically different than men; dare I not say superior... Yet, where is the empathy, consideration or space to experience the pain and suffering which can naturally occur during the physical changes that a girl to young woman, or mother to seasoned woman experiences? Almost non-existent.

They (men) will associate any shortcoming with our gender. When he makes a mistake, it's someone else's fault; when a woman makes a mistake, it must be that time of the month. If you're having a bad day, it must be your hormones. If you speak up about a problem in an assertive manner, you are being bossy. It's ridiculous and real.

Without going into all of the relatable particulars, we are charged with balancing quite a lot, unique to our gender. They are physical changes, emotional fluctuations, family planning dynamics, medical complications which can occur with stages of life, and often being treated in an inferior manner. It's unfortunate and unfair, yet reality.

Women often handle conflict differently, and want to massage situations to make it more palatable because we are nurturers by nature. It can be agonizing when our feelings are in the forefront. It's important to approach situations by being direct and then come back through with empathetic support. Your handling of situations needs to be rooted in the facts (data or metrics); as it's hard to argue with results (the work product). One of the best things you can do is to put standards over feelings, even when you are facing double standards.

Finally, while your success is certainly in your court, I debated including the male/female content because I don't like what's happening in the overall climate and culture. Yet, if you are to move with or without the ball, you need to level the playing field to your advantage whenever you can.

Knowing what's happening gives you the opportunity to strengthen and fortify yourself.

You deserve to win!

The Leader Within

So many things will be said about this moment in history. It's hard to believe it is only a blip of eternity. As a school leader, I have been trained to identify talent of all sorts and to tap leaders and assist them with growing in their leadership capacity. Leaders take on many forms and have different styles. Organizational charts tend to be the way we communicate to others leadership based off of rank and title. In grad school we learned of situational leadership, authoritarian, facilitative, etc., which was helpful and added perspective.

Often we attempt to categorize (without labeling, which gets a bit sticky) a person in hopes of better understanding who they are, and therefore what they will produce. It is also helpful for the leader to be familiar with the styles of those that work with them so that they can intentionally build a team comprised of varying personality types to best achieve the organizational goals.

As a little girl, I grew up in a single parent home. My mom began to teach me how to lead at a very young age by entrusting me with household chores and responsibilities. She instilled in me that when something is put in your charge, you should always take care of and do "it" at the highest level possible. As I grew older, I began to understand the interconnectedness of my small tasks (washing dishes, folding clothes, making the grocery list, making my bed, etc.) to the overall prosperity of our family.

My mother, who was the CEO of our home, modeled for me the importance of communicating clearly one's expectations, monitoring the quality of completion and then either correcting or praising us for our contribution. No one can do it all and even if you can, a true leader thinks about, *"Who's got next?"* and *"Have I prepared them?"*

One of the few constants in life is change. Recently, I visited a few of my favorite thought leaders for change and was reminded that those of us who lean in and embrace the opportunities that exist are the most successful on the other side. The strength of our endeavors lies in the leadership that is within all of us.

Move

It is so easy to shy away from the heart conversation, conflict and controversy, but I encourage you to learn to lean into love. Instead of shutting down, engage in meaningful conversations, learning opportunities, work sessions... and laugh together. Times like these require radical love.

Love shows itself in many ways, leadership is one. It's your time, Move. No need to wait on what or who is to come. Move now. Our futures are depending on it. There is plenty of room for us all to contribute to the conversation and move into action. Don't forget to love one another and then to continue to love one another. Love admits fault and forgives. Love is patient. Love is kind. It rights all wrongs. It is the work of any organization, group or family. That is how you persevere. It is how you conquer. It is how you win. Move!

Section Two
Preparing Our Children and (You) Parents for Successful Sports Careers

I'm a "Momager" what else can I say?

Passing the Ball in this context means being prepared and informed. Not all learned lessons must be lived. One of my big goals is to help young women to expedite their process so they can move much faster.

Women's Sports is finally getting noticed and here we are... And we are here to stay.

As the mother of female athletes, I'm sharing this section for you and for any young woman you know - to support the tactics/moves necessary for success - and my sincere hope is that you learn to live by them...

Sports also means business. It's time to navigate the Big Moves!

Who Was Going to Get Up?

The spring following my freshman season, I laid on the floor in the rec center on Saint Louis University's campus after working out, doing deep introspection. I chose this school when everyone was knocking on my door. This first year had been a huge disappointment. The big questions that kept circling in my head were, *Had I made the right decision? Am I cut out for this? Should I stay or should I go? Transfer or remain a member of the Lady Billikens?* Arrogance and cockiness responded first.

The coach said I would play! I'm the hometown favorite. Have you seen my trophy display, and all the records hanging in the halls of my high school? **What is wrong with you?**

My true self responded next. Get up and put in the work. Out work every woman on the roster. Be the undeniable choice not just to play, but to start. I decided to stay and work my way into the starting lineup.

Who was getting up?

My true self got up, with perspective, while the ball was not in my hand. It was the first time the realization had hit me - I was going to have to face the fact that I wouldn't play forever. What would happen next? I had never considered quitting before, as playing basketball had been such an integral part of my being and life. I wasn't ready to Move Without the Ball. I did the work...

Getting Up Again

I was laying on the floor during a game at West Pine Gym. Unlike a few months prior, it was not by choice. After accomplishing what I said and winning a spot in the starting lineup, *having the game of my career to date, I get a steal and am dribbling fast to the basket for a fast break layup. I jump*

off my right leg the way I had done thousands of times before and mid jump my knee buckles. I fall to the ground in instant pain followed by immediate numbness.
I let out a scream of heartbreak and fear so loudly that my husband rushed to the floor. I knew, he knew, everyone in the gym was silent because they knew too. ACL!

I laid there for a minute to compose myself before limping down to the trainer. Through examination, the injury was confirmed. I went to get an MRI and then scheduled surgery as soon as possible. I had to ask myself the same question I had asked not too long before. Who is getting up, why and how?

These became phoenix experiences for me (meaning I learned through my pain and heartbreak, how to rise from the ashes.) These were some of the significant ones I can readily discuss that have reoccurred in different ways throughout my life.

Whether you played sports or not, *can you relate to those moments in your life when you had to decide whether to stay down or rise?*

We have to learn that we fall down, but we can get back up again.

When you commit to reinventing yourself, self-regeneration daily, then, and only then will you have mastered *Moving Without the Ball.*

> *"Not only am I back, but I am better."*
> *- ShaCarri Richardson*

Building Success for (Elite) Athletes Abbreviated Questionnaire

Preparing your athlete takes a plan of action, focus, discipline, building strong skills, character and resilience, among other things. It's time to be objective and transparent about who you are, and what you have to offer!

Who are you as an athlete and what is an important goal for the short and long term? Identify by listing the traits of an elite athlete.

Trait #1_____   **Trait #2**_____

1. What is one behavior that shows you are working to improve on this trait daily?

2. What is one behavior you need to eliminate that is out of alignment with this trait?

3. How will you know that you have optimized this trait?

1. What is one behavior that shows you are working to improve on this trait daily?

2. What is one behavior you need to eliminate that is out of alignment with this trait?

3. How will you know that you have optimized this trait?

Name someone in professional sports who has star quality._____

On a scale of 1 to 4 (with 1 being I need a lot of support and 4 I am on the move!) rate yourself in the areas of:

Skill Level	1	2	3	4
Attitude	1	2	3	4
Coachability	1	2	3	4
Work Ethic	1	2	3	4
Commitment to self & team	1	2	3	4
Passion for athletic success	1	2	3	4
Moving without the ball	1	2	3	4

Winning in Life is Bigger than Sports

Ultimately we want our Student Athletes to win in life, not just games. That takes passion, skill, coach ability, commitment, communication, teamwork, discipline, accountability, perseverance, resilience, academic fortitude, ethical behavior, selflessness, and follow-through. I know that's a long list, but that's what it takes - that and even more. Student athletes also need to understand that at times the group/family is bigger than the individual.

The Top 11 Things Parents Need to Know about Preparing their Elite Student Athletes:

1.   **Don't try to live vicariously through your children. It's their life.**

2.   **Time Commitment** - Everything you want to become good at takes practice. On the road to being an elite athlete, expect to spend at least 20 hours a week between training, practice and competition.

3.   **Sacrifice** - it's a financial investment but also a sacrifice of your time and your schedule. Life will revolve around the student athlete's season... which means all seasons... pre-season, in season, post season and holidays.

        Tournaments become family vacations as well.

4.   **Vet the Coaches/Environment** - Student Athletes are impressionable and want to please and get the approval of their coach. The coach has a huge influence on their players.

29

Their work ethic should align with the family goal you set for your student athlete as well as their moral compass. You want someone who is more about what's in it for the student athlete rather than what's in it for them.

Instilling life principles - just because your student athlete is good doesn't mean they should be allowed to get away with just anything.

5. **Skill-based Placement is Essential** - The student athlete needs to play in order to get better - if that means they play at the YMCA to improve skills instead of on a club team, then they need to do so. No one gets better from sitting on the bench. That may mean dropping down from a club sport team to a rec team. It would be similar to playing junior varsity if you're not going to be able to earn playing time or contribute minute-wise to the varsity team.

6. **All sports and no fun leads to burnout.** If your student athlete quits because they are burned out, all of the sacrifice, investment and time is wasted. Make time for them to have fun - not sports related fun.

They need to take breaks because exhaustion can also lead to injury. Though they are young, their bodies still need rest and recovery. The game needs to be fun. All work and no play makes all of us grumpy.

7. **Explore multiple sports** - It's tempting to specialize in a sport; however, you don't know what your children are most naturally talented in if they don't explore other sports.

Also, cross training is good for the body as different muscles are activated and strengthened – this helps to prevent boredom and burnout.

8. **Manage their ego while protecting their self-esteem.** In the age of social media, they can be swayed by the comments, good or bad. As their parent, you must give them honest, balanced feedback. When they perform exceptionally, be their #1 cheerleader. When they perform poorly, be their #1 constructive critic, wrapped in love and care. If you don't do that well, you're creating a monster; either... kids who have an over inflated perception of themselves; or one who has esteem issues - lacking self-awareness, developing anxiety, or depression... all of which can lead to under developing their potential and ultimate success. Don't allow your elite student athlete's identity to be defined by the sport.

9. **Always demand their best effort** - giving 100%. The difference between going from good to great is being someone who separates themselves from the pack by pressing on. The 100% looks different from day to day. You eliminate regret when you give your best!

10. **Prioritize school before sports.** Do not allow your student athlete to sacrifice their grades for sports. Parents need to bring the same energy or more for school work, attendance, studying and exams. If the grade point average is not up to par, their scholarship choices will be limited.

11. **Seek advice from trusted sources.** Those who have gone through this process before you can offer lessons learned, how to avoid pitfalls, give recommendations, offer referrals and offer encouragement. This can accelerate you - allowing you to reclaim your time, money, heartache and momentum.

Never forget - youth sports is a business.

Be realistic about your student athlete's level of talent.

You can pay to play but it doesn't make them talented.

Don't be a victim of the market's making money game.

Some wins are not good wins - parents and student athletes need to remember that there are forces/people who are waiting and willing to corrupt individuals, if given the opportunity.

7 Ways to Prepare for Being an Athlete's Parent

1. **Don't take it personal** - when folks are heckling your child from the stands and you want to set them straight, use restraint. Remember, it's a part of the game. Especially when your child is outshining the rest, competition can breed contempt. Don't allow this to pull you out of character.

2. **Allow coaches to coach** - This ties back to vetting; once you've done that, you have to trust that they are making the best decisions in the moment.

3. **Elite Athletics is very expensive.** Decide how and where you will shift funds to accommodate the expenses. You don't want being on the team to become a burden. It should be a fun time for the family. When money is tight, it can cause tension. Planning ahead is essential.

4. **Maximize practice time for yourself** - it's easy to feel like you are being held hostage when your student athlete is practicing. Choose what you'll do, be it quiet time, exercising, making a grocery list, studying or completing work. If you have little ones, it might be a good time to offer homework help. There is only so much time in the day.

5. **Cultivate relationships with other parents** - Parents are all on the same team, just like our athletes, get used to it... Surprise, they ARE your new friends. Communicating, sharing transportation, building trust, responsibilities and being supportive to each other, your student athletes, and the general culture of the team lives with the parents. Cohesive parents often execute fundraisers, team dinners and other family activities together.

6. **Choose to enjoy being an "Uber" driver.** At whatever age, your student athletes will still need you to chauffer them, especially when you have multiple children, and after school.

    The whole evening may be filled with driving. Even after they are licensed drivers, your "services" may still be needed, as they may be extremely tired after intense practices, camps and day-long competitions.

7. **Find a way to make it a family affair.** - No one in your family should feel left out - because it is a lot. Your number one team should always be the home team. Be creative, finding ways to include each person in the family. You don't want one child overshadowing the other - it's easy to do. Don't do it.

Don't act up!
The scouts are looking at you in the stands just as they are observing your student athlete.
Your family is being recruited as well.

Preparing Student Athletes for Success On the Court and In Life

You and Your Parenting Behavior

Make no mistake parents, you are being observed and recruited too! How you behave in the stands, approach the coach after the game and/or demand your child's attention before, during and after a game are notable. Unless the coach is placing your child in danger, allow them to be the coach. If you do not trust or agree with the preparation and game plan strategy of the coaching staff, then the best option may be joining a different team.

When you display certain behaviors it models to your child that that is acceptable behavior. A coach understands that parents are a child's first and most influential teachers/coaches. Because they understand this to be true, attempting to rewire that level of programming is not a good assignment of resources, so they move on to the next recruit.

NIL Deals (Name, Image, Likeness - Student Athlete Compensation)

NIL has changed the recruitment process in ways that have totally transformed the collegiate space. We have all understood sports to be high revenue generating. However, I am not sure we truly understood how big this industry actually is in America. In 2022, college sports teams generated approximately $13.6 billion.

This (sports) is a business. In business there is always a bottom line, with the goal of profit. *When talent fails to produce, then they are cycled out.* Never have a conversation with the coach about your child getting more playing time.

The conversation should be about whether your child has the skill or potential to play at the level they are competing. If the honest assessment is that they are not, then drop down a level in order to play.

Getting better requires getting off the bench and into the game. Consider dynamics beyond the court/playing field which must be managed.

1. Social Media Presence

In today's world, everyone is on some social media platform. It is both a blessing and a curse. The blessing is that people from all over the world have the opportunity to connect in unprecedented ways. For a student-athlete, this is an opportunity to celebrate competition, personal accomplishments and showcase successes. These platforms have created an opportunity for athletes who may have not been seen otherwise to garner the attention of recruiters.

The curse is that if someone decides to change his/her mind about who they are and what they want to do professionally, it can be difficult. Posts are forever out there for the world to see. A high stake environment can have serious impact on opportunities as well as esteem. The comments that are made about posts can be uplifting and feel good or detrimental and cause anxiety, depression and/or stress.

I recommend that parents always monitor their student-athletes' accounts. I strongly discourage student-athletes from reading the comments so performance and purpose are not determined by external voices. Student-athletes receive plenty of feedback from trusted sources (family members, trainers, evaluators, and coaches) so they do not need the extra noise. Protect your peace and the peace of your child.

2. Nutrition/Diet

Garbage in, garbage out. It was so revealing for me to get to a point where I actually made the connection between nutrition and performance. I am actually very embarrassed that it took so long because it is common sense.

Think about nutrition from the perspective of owning a high priced car. In order to maintain the car and get the absolute optimal performance, you have to be very selective about the oil and gasoline which you allow to circulate through the engine. So it is with our bodies.

Planning meals that are balanced, remember the food groups, and appropriate portions is how we optimize performance. As your student-athlete progresses and grows in the game, I recommend scheduling a meeting with a dietician who can educate them around the number of calories that should be eaten daily and in what areas for the performance they seek.

3. Rest

Each and every one of us need to get our rest. In this instance I am speaking of sleep. It is recommended that teens (14–17 years) should get 8–10 hours of sleep each night. A good night's sleep goes a long way. Set a bedtime for yourself and your student-athlete so they are able to function at their highest level in the classroom and on the court.

4. Know the Difference between Being Recruited and Being Sold *"Organized Sports"* is a business.

Youth sports have increasingly become more about generating revenue than developing character and instilling middle class beliefs. Yet building core values is still happening, and if your child is on a team where it is absent, move on.

Youth sports is so entrenched in generating money, chasing money and spending money!

What parent who invests their time, funds and energy into practices, travel and competition, completely surrendering their personal schedule, doesn't want their child to be the "next" big star? Not one.

Here is a moment of transparency: Not all kids are as good as the coach says! Which is why I am telling you this here and now: Receiving an invitation to attend a camp, showcase or tournament does not necessarily mean your child is being recruited; they may be being 'sold.' Think about the weekly advertisements that still come in the mail. Those ads are a business's opportunity to sell something to you while making you believe they are giving you something.

This is *Marketing 101*. They market to your children the same way; to "sell" to your family in order to generate revenue. When your child has truly risen to the ranks of a recruit, anything the recruiter can give them for free, they will.

'Free' includes time, phone conversations, visits to campus, invitations with waived registration fees, etc., along with a financial offer of scholarship and yes, payment!

5. Child's Training/Competition Calendar
In the business of competitive sports, there really is no such thing as 'out of season.' You are doing either pre-season workouts, in-season competition, or post-season training. Because this is true, having a clearly outlined calendar will help stay organized, and it will also assist with preventing injury and/or burnout.

Kids need time to just be kids! Making time to socialize with friends is a must. Block out designated times and have 'shutdown days' as a household. Shutdown days means no watching, referencing or participating in sports that day.

Doing this relieves stress, allows for fun, and gives your family a chance to regroup without the pressure of being concerned about competing.

Your child needs an established self-identity outside of being an athlete. Unexpected events can interrupt a planned sports career. The 'game' can end before they are ready for it to come to an end for any number of reasons: injury, opportunity, health crisis, peaked and then plateaued skill level and academic achievement, etc., can all be factors.

Your children need to know that they are a whole person regardless of their current/future sports status - and also how to *Move Without the Ball* in a mentally healthy space. This can only happen if they have been taught the multifaceted aspects that make them whole and complete. They are enough with or without the ball.

6. Camp Participation

Attending camps is a great way to focus on skill development, building relationships with the hosts school, and a great way to be discovered. The coaches will not be able to deny the talent in front of them. So, if the student-athlete is seen as someone who can fill a need and contribute to the team, this could be their big break.

Select intentionally which schools/camps your child will attend. In the elementary up to middle school years, students should play as much as they can, when and where they are able.

In middle school up through high school, narrowing where to spend money for travel, food, hotel and miscellaneous items so that there is a return on investment becomes more critical. Most universities recruit in their home and surrounding states, for fiscal reasons. Make sure your local universities are on your list.

Recruiters also have budgets, costs and expenses, which is why they tap the talent in their region unless they have a superstar who wants to come to their school who will be a game changer!

Since you now know how they recruit, let that knowledge guide which camps you attend.

Finally, think about your children's personal brand. They are likely most recognizable in their community. Choosing schools that are proximal to your permanent address and/or family base will assist with NIL deals and perhaps even playing time, as boosters get a vote.

7. Academic Achievement

Keep the books in front of the ball. The reason we call them student-athletes is because you have to be a student, first, in order to be an eligible student-athlete. There are unlimited stories about top players not being able to go to the next level due to academic struggles.

We also must remember that at some point everyone has to eventually transition out of their athletic career. Some sooner or later than others, but everyone will transition. That is why I must emphasize the importance of keeping first things first. I am an educator so this is super near and dear to my heart. I tell people all of the time, as someone who knows what sports can do in the life of a child, who feels as if sports saved my life, I still stress books then ball.

Academic Success

The same way you have a practice routine, student-athletes need a study hall routine. Building the habit of time management that includes hitting the books is an essential skill for all student athletes at any level.

As the student-athlete advances to higher education, it is common to miss classes due to road trips. In those stretches, good study habits really pay off. The team may or may not have set study hall time, but when they are on the charter bus or plane that is a great time to buckle down and get classwork done or simply study.

Falling behind is so easy; yet it's very hard to recover from, as the semester blows by fast.
Most high school and collegiate programs have grade checks built into their program. If a student is in academic jeopardy, a tutor is provided as an intervention along with scheduled study hall time that is documented at a designated location.

If grades continue to decline, the student athlete may be suspended from the team in order to focus only on academic achievement for a period of time.

The worst case scenario is a student athlete losing eligibility and not being able to remain on the team's roster at all. Heartbreaking from the competition aspect, especially at the college level, losing scholarship eligibility will have financial ramifications. Without tuition, room, board or extras, heading home and figuring out a new pathway is likely the option. How will they complete their education? How will they Move Without the Ball?

A Note About Women and Girls in Sports

Women's/Girls' Sports are Different - Just as issues/challenges and physical constraints are in the workplace, challenges faced by women in sports include --- sexual harassment, discrimination, pay disparity, subpar accommodations (lodging, competition and training facilities, transportation, meals, etc.), marketing that over emphasizes sensuality of the athlete above superior skill set in the sports.

While change won't come immediately, we are at a unique crossroad where we have a real chance of transforming the environment.

Methods to Move the Obstacles

- Unionizing to have a collective of people who will speak against inequities

- Refusing to accept certain conditions

- Sharing data that reveals market interest and fan support for the sport

- Working hard to continue taking the sport to the next level, along with your own individual game

- Calling out individuals/organizations who cross the line and holding the industry/persons accountable

Section Three

The Endgame is Success

Building unshakeable self-belief begins by connecting to
your BURN.
This requires Leveling Up.

I was an accountant before I became a teacher. I left that job
because I preferred people over spreadsheets. Honestly, the
work was not difficult, but the job wasn't fulfilling to me. I
decided to become a teacher because I wanted to be around
people and it was an opportunity to interact...

Perhaps you can relate?

You may be considering your next move.

What do you want to do and what environment would
be your preference?

What are potential limitations and great opportunities?

Transitions

Earlier, I mentioned playing basketball professionally, and internationally. I'd had hopes and dreams of becoming a WNBA player, and at one point felt international professional basketball was a bridge to getting there. I played for one season and then I had to come to terms with the fact that my skill level wasn't going to get me recruited into the WNBA. Sure, I could have played another season... But the sacrifices did not match up to the potential rewards.

There is a certain amount of confidence an established player has when they are part of the team. But, what about when it's over? When it's time to transition to a career or new endeavor in life, like achieving another degree or certification? The emotion, the effort and the resources are needed to make this transition successfully, and it can be difficult.

As women in professional settings and leadership roles, we often measure decisions based on our families and careers when making complex choices. It's different for us because we are typically the caregivers and are judged harshly for choosing our careers over traditional family structures.

Facing and Overcoming Limitations

Personal assessment requires aligning your goals to your skillset and facing the realities of your capability, and capacity. If you are not able to be honest about your abilities, it only delays the inevitable. Think about it: You want to become a public speaker but you have paralyzing stage fright; that's not likely going to work out.

You desire to become an Olympic sprinter, but you're slow as a turtle.

You desire to be an engineer, but struggle with upper level math classes.

You want to be a Fire Chief, but struggle to carry your body weight though you're strong. You're not as strong as you need to be to rescue someone out of a burning building.

Career Path

On a professional and personal level, it's important to reflect on what you actually want, what areas you excel in, and to then commit to discovery...

What do you want? Think about it - flexibility, pay, work environment, colleagues, equity, opportunity for advancement, harmony...

There's good news! Through exploration and discovery, you can become clear about who you are, where you are and in what areas you may likely find your greatest success.

Taking the time to explore these questions is similar to shopping for a new apartment, vehicle or house - you know the attributes, you know your style and you know your budget... and when you search, you begin to find things you hadn't considered and also cross things off that you may not be able to envision or cannot accomplish in this moment...

When employers are hiring, they post a job description that includes the role, responsibilities and experience - they do a good job of describing, but what is not said is about: Reliability, dedication, passion, accountability, positive attitude, etc. These are the attributes that are often assessed during the interview process after the candidates have been screened.

Here are some pointers for your consideration:

Vision for Your Future - What would you like to do long term? What industry, service or other?

Interests - Do you wish to be in the educational field, service industry, and business or perhaps begin an entrepreneurial endeavor?

Transferable Skills - What (experiences) did you have in school/past positions, which might be helpful in the future?

Experience - What else have you done that might be helpful? Hobbies, volunteerism, etc.

Marketability - Do you have a bio/resume or other that captures who you are in this moment, and where you hope to move?

Write down the attributes you need to feel successful:

Attributes Of My Success Vision

To assist you in answering these questions, please complete the assessments and let's see where they take us as we *Move Without the Ball...* We're getting ready for the Burn!

Move Without the Ball
Pre-Assessment

Moving without the ball requires you to make a mind shift. Every action we take starts in our minds. Our beliefs will drive our behaviors and our behaviors will become our habits. Leaders in sports and life understand the importance of setting themselves up for success by readying their minds to do the work.

Let's take a few moments to determine where you are and where you want to move. Take this pre-assessment to rate yourself over the last year in each category using the numbers 1-5. 1 means you rarely do it and 5 means you do it all of the time.

No --- to ---Yes	1	2	3	4	5
I believe that I can accomplish anything I set my mind to.					
I have a purpose or passion that I connect to daily to drive my actions.					
I have a core set of values that help me keep perspective when things get hard or I face a setback/adversity.					
I have a strong and clear vision of the person I want to be in my life.					
I have a solid and trackable routine that is activity based and not just focused on getting "results."					
I have complete clarity on what I want my LEGACY to be.					
I have cultivated an environment that fully supports my goals and values.					
Overall, I feel that I have a good foundation of mental toughness.					
TOTAL					
FINAL SCORE					

8-15 Needs to do some pre-work	16-23 Showing	24-31 Ready to move	32-40 On the Move

Achieving Your Vision Takes Adjusting

Coaches can guide and support your adjustments, leading to greater success.

You have to be clear on your goal (vision for yourself), you need a (game plan) blueprint and a group of people who support getting you there... formally in sports, it could be a coach, manager, agent, trainer, teammates. Informally in sports and in life, it could be parents, family members, partner or spouse, friends, coworkers, mentor, pastor, or an actual coach.

One of the biggest questions we ask ourselves in this life is *Who am I and what am I purposed for?* On the journey to discover the answer to these questions, I have found it important to become self-aware enough to follow the paths that will lead you to your answer. One of the clues I have learned to leverage is something, one of the top ranked mental performance coaches in the world, Ben Newman, calls The Burn.

In sports, one often hears 'feel the burn.' That phrase means that you have put in enough repetitions with weight training, cardio or exertion to be close to the point of exhaustion. It is said as if feeling the pain or tingle in your muscles is an indication of expansion, strengthening and growth. Well, as it relates to life, we must also feel The Burn.

That burn is what will get you up to go in to a difficult work situation. It is the feeling in the pit of your stomach that tells you not to quit, as the reward is just on the horizon.

It is important to distinguish the difference between the BURN and your WHY. One is a feeling and the other a knowing.

Both are important, but sometimes knowing isn't enough. As someone who chose to go into the field of education, my why was that I believe all students no matter what zip code they are born deserve to receive a quality education. My Burn however, is that my grandmother who grew up in the Jim Crow South was not allowed to go to the same quality of schools as white children, so I have a value for how accessibility to a high quality education correlates to future life outcomes. I feel it is every child who is born in America's right to have access to a quality free appropriate public education knowing that free appropriate public education is not always quality.

Being clear on your vision for yourself is the first step to getting in touch with The Burn and knowing your why so that a blueprint can be created both as a game plan for success in sports and life.

Who are you going to need on your team to accomplish your goals? How are you going to help others by accomplishing your goals? What does support look like as far as helping you get there?

Some days you may need to hear a hard truth from a teammate/ colleague, coach/supervisor about your performance. On other days, you will cherish the positive feedback that comes from these same people.

Early in the morning as you are making a decision whether to put in a little more work or stay in bed or late at night trying to decide whether to go to sleep or watch just one more episode, your support might come from an accountability partner in the form of your parent, children, partner or spouse.

The point is that we all need trusted advisors surrounding us and cheering us to the next level as we make moves in this life, and that is what I call a coach.

Coaches can be for personal or professional benefit. They may serve dual/multiple roles in your life. What I believe distinguishes a coach from everyone else is that they are invested in your development for the sole purpose of your growth, development and improvement. The results may lead to collective advancement, but even when the metrics don't translate for the group, you the individual are better. All of us should have a coach.

I am grateful for the ones I have had and those who currently sit in that seat, making sure I continue to *Move Without the Ball.*

Get you one - it will transform your life for the better forever!

The Burn

No matter what industry or discipline has brought you to this playbook, your next level must begin by addressing the belief you have in yourself. Building unshakeable self-belief begins by connecting to your BURN. Here you can set the foundation by helping you connect to your Burn and revealing the *Five Key Factors for Attaining Belief in Yourself.* This is going to require you to be honest with yourself and your story. Be vulnerable, be present, be where your feet are. *Let'* move.

Let's inspect and craft a belief system to build upon. Everything you do in life stems from your belief system. Now, I'm not going to tell you what to believe, but we are going to take a deeper look into your mindset. Top performers in both business, sports and life have something that drives them to greatness. And, it goes deeper than just their why or their purpose. The Burn is what really lights them up to believe anything is possible. It's the mindset that causes them to fight on a different level. I'm a firm believer that the same Burn lies inside each and every single one of us. When we uncover it and connect to it on a consistent basis, it will light our why on fire and drive us to Move Without the Ball. The Burn in your heart, that underlying passion will help us fight through anything in life and emerge on a different plane than that of where we started. My deep inner passion is to constantly become the best version of myself.

If it's going to be a goal or something you're fighting for, once you reach it, you must redefine and reconnect to something deeper. That being said, it's also okay if your Burn changes over time based on your different stages of life, adversities you may face, etc. This is not rocket science. There is no equation to finding the perfect Burn, and it's not something you are glued to from here on out. I reserve the right to change my mind, and you should learn that too. It is so freeing!

All that matters is you understand your Burn and connect to it daily. With that you will create an environment that drives accountability and causes you to do what it takes. This is about attacking the next level and becoming your best self.

The Burn ignites it all. Use this area to brainstorm ideas of what you think your Burn might be...

Five Factors to Attaining Belief in Yourself

True mental toughness starts with attaining belief in yourself. I'm not talking about the surface level belief or happy go-lucky positivity. I'm talking about honest and deeply rooted foundational belief that is based on the truth.

1. **Accept the Truth**
    Realizing and identifying with the person you are today is the key to becoming the person you want to be. Remember this: we never actually fail in life. We just don't always get the results that we want. You cannot live a lie. You have to acknowledge and identify with what is most important in your life to ultimately, "Attain Belief in Yourself."

2. **Speak the Truth**
    You may be reluctant – even scared – to talk about or acknowledge past behavior and habits that you regret. However, avoiding it only serves to amplify the pain and make us feel like victims. Get the truth out into the light by talking about your experiences with a trusted friend or a professional.

3. **Breathe Through the Truth**
    Even though every fiber of your being wants to react by believing that your actions up to this point have been correct, know that you can change. Avoid acting from a place of pain or anger. The best way to reclaim your dignity is to behave rationally and treat yourself lovingly – which will keep you from self-destructing.

4. **Process the Truth**
    Give yourself time and space to find your equilibrium. Believe confidently and whole-heartedly that making these changes will prompt you to develop a stronger foundation. However, recognize that this will take time – and give yourself that time.

5. **Create a Plan Based on the Truth**
Don't expect things to be perfect right away; you can't simply flip a switch and have a new life. Old behaviors and mindsets often come back into the realm. Stay strong and acknowledge that you must continue to believe and actively engage in this process in order to experience concrete change for your future. With this in mind, define how do you want to live your life from now on.

Use this section to really think through what you want out of your life. Open your heart and mind and dump it onto this worksheet below. Don't hold yourself back. Think BIG and get extremely clear on exactly what YOU write down in each of the boxes. This is the foundation of your work. Let's move!

YOUR BURN

PERSONAL GOALS

PROFESSIONAL GOALS

The Burn Journal Challenge

Now that you've explored your Burn, I have a challenge for you. Over the next 30 days, I want you to challenge yourself to connect to your unique Burn every single day using what I call, "The Burn Journal Challenge." Now, you can use a physical journal (how I do it) or you can start a journal in your phone - whatever works for you. Every morning for the next 30 days you're going to write your Burn in this journal and connect to it. This will help you decide if the Burn you wrote down is powerful enough, or if you need to dig a little deeper. When you've truly uncovered what your current Burn is, you will be flooded with energy and passion to take the necessary action in your daily life. Your greatest level of performance relies on your ability to connect to your true Burn.

Step 1: Your Alarm
I'm not saying you have to wake up the same time I do every day, but whenever you set your alarm clock, go in and rename the alarm to your Burn. Mine says "Make a Move, Jana." After seeing that, I lock in, and I'm ready to *Move Without the Ball.*

Step 2: The Journal
Grab a small journal or notebook and commit to writing down your Burn every morning for the next 30 days. This is what I mean by "connecting" to your Burn.
This will help you build the environment that it takes to consistently connect to this inner FIRE and allow it to light up your actions to a whole new level of consistency.

Move Without the Ball
Post-Assessment

Optimally, give yourself 30, 60 and 90 days to measure your progress. Take the post-assessment below and rate yourself in each category using the scale 1-5 at each interval. This will connect you to what you have learned and prepare you for your next level of GREATNESS, be ready to make the moves that will catapult you to success in sports and life.

No --- to ---Yes	1	2	3	4	5
I strongly believe that I can accomplish anything I set my mind to.					
I have uncovered my purpose or passion, "BURN" that I connect to daily to drive my actions.					
I have a core set of values that help me keep perspective AND reframe when things get hard or I face a setback/adversity.					
I have a strong and clear vision of the person I want to be in my life.					
I have a solid and trackable routine that is activity based and not just focused on getting "results."					
I have complete clarity on what I want my LEGACY to be.					
I have identified and made adjustments to my environment that will support my path to success.					
I have cultivated an environment that fully supports my goals and values.					
I have a clear ACTION PLAN that is in alignment with the life I want to build and the person I want to become.					
Overall, I feel that I have a good foundation of mental toughness.					
TOTAL					
FINAL SCORE					

8-15 Needs to do some pre-work	16-23 Showing	24-31 Ready to move	32-40 On the Move

The content in this section was adapted from Ben Newman's *Mental Toughness Playbook.*

Want to learn more about **The Burn?** Contact Dr. Jana Haywood at Illuminesolutionsgroupisg.com to sign-up for the *Mental Toughness Playbook Series.*

Words of Wisdom

"You miss 100% of the shots you don't take."
–Wayne Gretzky

Life really is a school full of lessons uncovered through trial and error. The greatest to do this game of life understand that turnovers, errors and mistakes are all a part of the process. I am learning even now that some of my most beautiful life lessons have come when I literally thought the sky was falling on top of me.

Becoming stronger and better through what we learn is a key to success in sports and life. All is well, even when it's tough. Don't linger too long when our assignments are for a time. Celebrate the victories. Treat setbacks as setups and learning opportunities. Do not be the person who keeps making the same mistake; do something different and just maybe you will find what you are looking for. Every experience we have is leading us to the next and none of them are wasted.

In the famous Pixar animation film, *Finding Nemo*, Dory repeatedly says, "Just keep swimming." When Nemo felt like giving up and the task appeared insurmountable, he remembered those words of wisdom and kept swimming.

In one of my favorite children's books, a little engine comes to a point where what it believes about its ability to accomplish a huge task was true if it thought it could, or if it thought it couldn't. That little engine with all of its gusto and might, chants as it pulls, "I think I can. I think I can," and does.

In this moment, I want to tell you, "Just keep moving." Believing something is one thing but doing something is altogether different. As a person thinks, so are they.

Success begins in your thoughts and is made manifest by the miracles all around us. Success is on the path as we *Move Without the Ball.*

Blessings to you on your journey.

Let's move!

"Our deepest fear is not that we are inadequate. Our deepest fear is that we are powerful beyond measure. It is our light, not our darkness that most frightens us. We ask ourselves, 'Who am I to be brilliant, gorgeous, talented, fabulous?' Actually, who are you not to be? You are a child of God. Your playing small does not serve the world. There is nothing enlightened about shrinking so that other people won't feel insecure around you. We are all meant to shine, as children do. We were born to make manifest the glory of God that is within us. It's not just in some of us; it's in everyone. And, as we let our own light shine, we unconsciously give other people permission to do the same. As we are liberated from our own fear, our presence automatically liberates others."

- This quote is originally from the book A Return to Love: Reflections on the Principles of a Course in Miracles by Marianne Williamson.

About the Author

Dr. Jana Haywood was inducted into the St. Louis Sports Hall of Fame in 2018. She has been inducted into the Lutheran North High School Hall of Honor twice; once individually and the other with the 1997-1999 State Track and Field Championship Teams.

Jana was an outstanding student and athlete while at Lutheran North High School in St. Louis, MO. While attending, she competed at the varsity level in three sports: cross-country, basketball and track. She was a member of a three-peat women's track & field state championship teams (set a state record in the high jump), quarterfinals in state basketball, and advanced to the state championship for two years in cross-country. Jana was the metropolitan area-scoring leader in basketball multiple seasons. She was also the St. Louis Post-Dispatch Student Athlete of the Year.

Jana continued her athletic career at Saint Louis University with a four-year scholarship in basketball. She was co-captain of the team in 2003 and 2004. While she was playing at SLU, the women's team advanced for the first time to the WNIT. Her basketball skills took her around the world: Puerto Rico, Italy, Spain and France.

She graduated from Saint Louis University with a Bachelor of Science in Accounting and Human Resources. She continued her education at Fontbonne University with a Master of Arts in Education and Special Education. She also received a Master of Arts in Educational Administration from Lindenwood University. She culminated her studies earning a Doctor of Education in Leadership from Maryville University.

Jana started her career in education in 2005 in the St. Louis Public School District. Her Lutheran education instilled numerous core values with service being foundational. She found success by sharing her personal experiences as she shifted her focus from sports to eliminating barriers that negatively impact students' academic success, specifically those that disproportionately impact underserved and underrepresented communities. She presents at the Beyond Consequences Trauma-Informed Schools local and national conferences and serves on the advisory council for the Crisis Prevention Institute stressing the importance of de-escalation techniques that exclude restraint and seclusion of students with self-care as the anchor strategy.

She has worked as a teacher, athletic director, assistant principal and principal. In 2020, she was selected as the Enterprise Holdings Secondary School Leader of the Year. In 2021, she accepted the position as Principal of Ritenour High School in St. Louis County. Today she is the Assistant Superintendent of Human Resources in the Ferguson-Florissant School District. She also serves as an Adjunct Professor in the School of Education at Saint Louis University. Jana co-founded Illumine Solutions Group, a coaching and consulting company with her husband to ignite, inspire and empower people as they pursue their personal goals.

Jana is a member of Washington Tabernacle MB Church. She serves on the Julia B. Hattitude Scholarship Fund Committee. She is a Board Member for Dream Builders 4 Equity.

Her husband is Carl Haywood Jr. and together they have three children; Carl, Jaila, and Jordyn.

www.ingramcontent.com/pod-product-compliance
Lightning Source LLC
Chambersburg PA
CBHW051239120626
46547CB00014B/1709